Original title:
The Great Meaning of Life Scavenger Hunt

Copyright © 2025 Creative Arts Management OÜ
All rights reserved.

Author: Maxwell Donovan
ISBN HARDBACK: 978-1-80566-265-5
ISBN PAPERBACK: 978-1-80566-560-1

The Puzzle of the Universe

Jigsaw pieces in the sky,
Stars misplaced, oh my, oh my!
Galaxies chase their own tails,
While comets write hilarious tales.

Aliens play hide and seek,
Laughing as they peek and peek.
Gravity's just a silly prank,
Balancing on a spacey plank.

Constellations craft their jokes,
Tickling thoughts of distant blokes.
We're all just actors on a stage,
In this cosmic comedy page.

Quest for Authenticity

Ah, the search for staying real,
Wearing socks with sandals, what's the deal?
We strive for truth, yet squint to see,
If we're ourselves or just a meme.

Instagram filters rule the day,
Faking smiles in a staged array.
But authenticity's a dance,
Two left feet at every chance.

The mirror laughs with a sarcastic grin,
As our selfies scream, "Is this a win?"
Chasing mirrors all day long,
Wondering where we went wrong.

Harvesting Moments of Insight

In the garden of my mind,
Thoughts are sprouting, hard to find.
Weeding out the crazy fluff,
What's profound? It's all so tough!

Gathering wisdom like ripe fruits,
But it's mostly just wild roots.
Chickens scratch at deep thoughts,
Plucking wisdom! Oh, what a plot!

The scarecrow chuckles, full of zeal,
While I harvest my next big meal.
Moments baked in sunlight's glow,
Doused in absurdity's show.

Explorations in the Abyss

I peeked into the void down there,
Only to find a lost teddy bear.
Thought I'd solve the age-old riddle,
But came back laughing, feeling brittle.

Echoes of my own nonsense chatter,
"Why is existence such a platter?"
A bottomless pit of giggles and sighs,
Where philosophy wears clown disguise.

Grabbed a pizza slice of fate,
A cosmic meal shared with debate.
In the depths where thoughts take flight,
I danced with shadows, what a sight!

Hidden Gems of the Heart

In pockets deep, treasures hide,
A lost sock's mate, a friend's old guide.
The last piece of cake, oh what a find,
Life's little quirks are simply divine.

Under the couch, what's that? A shoe?
Exploring my house, it seems brand new.
Old toys and memories, scattered with glee,
In this zany hunt, I find ME!

Pathways of Enlightenment

A trail of crumbs, leading to bliss,
Forgotten snacks, oh how they entice!
The road of wisdom, paved in cheese,
Laughing at life, with a wink and a tease.

Hopscotch on dreams, with giggles and skips,
Chasing my tail, what a few mad trips!
Puns and jokes, scattered like sprinkles,
On this wild path, my heart simply twinkles.

Navigating the Maze of Meaning

Round and round, a dizzying chase,
Is that my reason? Or just my place?
Finding true north with a rubber duck,
In a maze of chaos, I'm just out of luck.

Trapdoors and surprises, oh what a scene,
Straight lines are boring, I'll stay in between.
Each twist and turn, a laugh and a fumble,
In this crazy puzzle, I will not stumble.

The Search for Essence

In search of cheese, I stumble and crawl,
The essence of joy, on my kitchen wall.
Is it found in laughs, or crumbs from a snack?
Searching for treasures, I'll not hold back.

A hint of silliness, tucked in my hat,
Oh, where is that essence? Maybe a cat?
Chasing her tail, she seems to know more,
In this wacky game, I'll always explore.

The Secret Garden of Meaning

In a garden filled with socks,
Where lost thoughts tickle rocks,
I found a key that wouldn't fit,
And a note that said, 'Not a bit!'

Butterflies flying in a line,
Chasing shadows, feeling fine,
I tripped on daisies, laughed a lot,
Found wisdom hiding in a pot!

The gnomes giggled at my quest,
Whispered secrets, never guessed,
They pointed high, to a tree so tall,
Promised meaning if I could just crawl!

Footprints in the Sand of Eternity

Walking along the beach of dreams,
Counted seagulls, plotting schemes,
Wrote my hopes in grains of sand,
Then a wave came, oh so bland!

Footprints danced in patterns odd,
A crab passed by, gave me a nod,
Each step led to paths unknown,
With flip-flops lost, I felt alone!

Time's a tide that pulls and drags,
Sometimes fun, but often sags,
Yet in this wandering footrace,
I found joy in every misplaced trace!

Tokens from the Journey

I carry tokens in my pack,
A rubber band, a tiny snack,
A paperclip with hopes attached,
And a joke that totally scratched!

The map is drawn in crayon bright,
With doodles that bring pure delight,
X marks a spot where I can sip,
Some fizzy juice, a quenchy trip!

Each trinket tells a funny tale,
Of missed buses and playful snail,
In this randomness, I find a spark,
Tokens shining bright, leaving a mark!

Searching for the Unseen

With a magnifying glass in hand,
I sought the wisdom, oh so grand,
Looked under beds, behind the chair,
Found a sock, but wisdom's rare!

I climbed a tree to reach the sky,
A squirrel scolded, oh my, oh my,
But in the branches, I lost my shoe,
Was that the sign? I never knew!

Chasing shadows, what a delight,
Misplaced laughter, all seemed right,
In the end, I found a scene,
Life's a puzzle, and I'm the glean!

Heartbeats in the Silence

In the whispers of the night, it seems,
We search for laughter in our dreams.
A sock that wanders, a shoe that plays,
Tickling our hearts in the silliest ways.

With each heartbeat, a clue we find,
Lost between the silly and the blind.
A giggle, a snort, a dance in the rain,
Life's secret treasures, again and again.

Chasing shadows of old lost toys,
Funny mischief, those childhood joys.
Searching for meaning in a peanut jar,
Each quirky find, a shining star.

So let's toast to the quirky and absurd,
In the chaos, find joy, so undeterred.
For in this hunt, we come alive,
In every heartbeat, we truly thrive.

Clues in the Canvas of Time

Time's a canvas, a splash of cheer,
With paint spills and laughter, take a beer.
A puzzle of crumbs and a twist of fate,
We find hidden gems on our dinner plate.

From scratchy records to funky socks,
Searching wisdom in our old lunch boxes.
Each doodle and smudge a riddle bold,
Tales of adventures yet to be told.

Time may tick, but we dance along,
In mismatched shoes, we sing our song.
Past and future merging in a twirl,
Finding joy in the oddest swirl.

So let's paint the world in shades of jest,
Each moment a clue, each laugh a quest.
In our masterpiece, let's forever roam,
With every stroke, we find our home.

Shadows of What Matters

In the shadows, we tiptoe with glee,
Chasing whispers of what we can't see.
A belly laugh behind a closed door,
Where fun and folly are bound to soar.

The cat is plotting, the dog has a scheme,
In their playful world, we dare to dream.
Every giggle an echo of things that matter,
In this silly chase, our hearts grow fatter.

Time slips away like a sneaky cat,
Pouncing on moments that make us flat.
Yet in those giggles, the truth will shine,
In this scavenger hunt, our lives align.

So dance with shadows, don't take a break,
Follow the laughter, for goodness' sake!
In the end, we'll find our light and bliss,
In every silly moment, we live in this.

Chasing Moments of Wisdom

We chase the moments, both big and small,
With a rubber chicken and a cardboard wall.
Wise old turtles with their secret laughs,
Guide us through life's incomprehensible paths.

Frogs jump high, dispensing their knowledge,
While squirrels debate in the grandest college.
Every giggle a nugget, every pun a sign,
In this treasure hunt, we're never confined.

Chasing the sun with a bucket of joy,
Swinging our arms as we find our ploy.
In puddles of laughter and lakes of delight,
We uncover chapter and verse of the bright.

So let's embrace every odd little quirk,
For wisdom's found where we play and smirk.
In the chase for the quirky, we find life's truth,
In the silly moments, we rediscover youth.

Echoes of Forgotten Sentences

In the attic lies a shoe,
Full of dust and old glue.
What secrets does it keep?
Or is it just a place to sleep?

A sock whispers jokes from the past,
With laughter that seemed to last.
If only I could hear them clear,
But maybe I'm just stuck right here.

The fridge hums a quirky tune,
Beeping like a wild raccoon.
It holds snacks in silent jest,
While I ponder what's for breakfast.

A spoon once danced under the night,
Stirring soup with all its might.
It twirled and spun with glee,
Until it got lost with the tea.

Mysteries in the Mundane

A fork fell down, who could it be?
Tripped on pasta, set it free!
It sparkled like a stolen star,
Claimed its throne, what a bizarre.

A pillow's full of dreams so bright,
Each one fades before the light.
Did I dream I was a knight?
Or just struggle with snacks at night?

The cat conducts a silent play,
With audience made of stray hay.
Whiskers twitch, eyes closed tight,
In their world, everything's right.

A sock puppet seeks a mate,
While pondering a grand debate.
Is life just one big sock slide?
Or a yarn of truth, we can't abide?

Light in the Labyrinth

Wandering through a maze of cheese,
From cheddar to brie, oh please!
A mouse gives tips on where to go,
But I'm blinded by pizza dough.

A map made of spaghetti strands,
Reveals the treasure in my hands.
Just follow the trail of crumbs,
To find life's jokes—not just the sums.

Each corner turned, a giggle lurks,
In the shadows, magic works.
The exit's near, or so they say,
But first, let's dance and play!

In this labyrinth of jokes and glee,
I trip on laughter, oh, woe is me!
Yet each misstep leads to delight,
In this maze, I find my light.

Journeying through the Infinite

On a bus made of jellybeans,
Traveling through laughter's scenes.
Each seat, a story waiting to share,
And every giggle fills the air.

The ticket collector's a wise old slug,
With a backpack that's full of hugs.
He charges smiles for the ride,
As we journey together side by side.

Clouds billow up like puffy cakes,
What silly shapes the universe makes!
A teapot floats, pouring out dreams,
While we sip from giggling streams.

At the end of this wacky spree,
Is the treasure of pure joy, you see?
Unraveling life, one chuckle at a time,
With each verse, I'm dancing in rhyme!

Cryptic Messages of the Universe

I found a sock inside a star,
It whispered secrets from afar.
A sandwich, too, with cosmic jam,
What's the meaning? Who gives a damn!

A rubber ducky floats on by,
It quacks in riddles, oh my my!
Each random thing has tales to share,
In this mixed bag of cosmic flair.

A spoon in orbit, lost in space,
It twirls and dances, what a race!
Collecting oddities so grand,
Their messages, hard to understand.

So grab your map, it's time to roam,
Through aisles of laughs, we'll find a home.
With each strange clue, we'll laugh and grin,
In this wild chase, we're sure to win!

The Dance of Intentions

Intentions tango through the night,
With chicken hats, oh what a sight!
They wobble and wobble in silly shoes,
Making decisions like penguin blues.

A rubber chicken leads the way,
Squeaking wisdom, hip-hip-hooray!
We'll cha-cha-cha through cotton candy,
Seeking truths that feel quite dandy.

At every turn, a pie may fly,
In this dance, we laugh and sigh.
We'll spin and twirl 'til dawn's first light,
Intentions wiggling, oh what a night!

So grab a partner, don't be shy,
In this zany waltz, we'll surely try.
To jiggle our way to dreams so fine,
With every boogie, we'll cross the line!

Beyond the Horizon of Ordinary

Past the hills of mundane sighs,
Where bananas wear a monkey disguise.
We'll chase the wind and talk to trees,
Gathering laughter like honeybees.

A kazoo plays a tune so bright,
Leading us toward another delight.
We'll jump on clouds and ride the breeze,
As ordinary fades with the greatest of ease.

In lands where socks and shoes can chat,
And time slows down for a polite cat.
We'll share our tales with a giggling brook,
In this funny world, take a look!

So venture forth, you brave, bold souls,
To silly lands where laughter rolls.
With each step, wisdom's found in fun,
As we embrace the unusual run!

Journeys in Search of Purpose

A turtle wearing boots, oh my!
He's on a quest, so spry and sly.
With each little step, he stops to snack,
On purpose pie, no turning back!

With a squirrel sidekick named Sir Chuck,
They navigate with wild, silly luck.
Every misstep leads to a joke,
In this strange search, no need to poke.

Along the way, a llama sings,
Dancing in circles, oh the joy it brings!
They gather stories from the trees,
With every laugh, they feel the breeze.

So pack your bags, don your hats,
Join the journey, laugh with the bats.
With every twist, we'll find our role,
In this wacky hunt for the hidden goal!

Insight Illuminated

Searching high, searching low,
For treasures that make us glow.
Dancing around with plastic spoons,
Under the light of goofy moons.

Chasing tails of rainbow cats,
While avoiding the hungry gnats.
Each clue is wrapped in silly jokes,
With giggles shared among the folks.

Finding socks instead of gold,
With secrets of the ages told.
In cereal boxes, we dive deep,
Unearthing dreams that make us leap.

A treasure map made out of cheese,
Leads us to mysteries with great ease.
We laugh and leap from plume to plume,
As joy explodes, dispelling gloom.

The Whisper of Ancient Echoes

Footsteps shuffle on dusty floors,
Echoes of laughter behind closed doors.
We throw confetti at the frowning past,
Collecting giggles, we're having a blast.

With each old scroll, a riddle unfolds,
Wrapped up in laughter, a tale unfolds.
A quest for smiles through time and space,
As grumpy statues provide us grace.

Banana peels slip us from fate,
Awkward falls—oh, how great!
Tickling roots of ancient trees,
We crown ourselves with leafy leaves.

Mapping the Ethereal

A compass spins, lost in the air,
Pointing us to who knows where.
Maps drawn in crayon, oh what a sight,
Guiding us through laughter each night.

Chasing shadows of giggling ghosts,
We toast marshmallows, giggle the most.
The stars are busy doing their thing,
While we dance and make the cosmos sing.

Fingerpainted skies, so bold and bright,
Charting the way with sheer delight.
Our hearts are markers, silver and gold,
Finding the warmth that never grows cold.

Crossroads of Discovery

At the crossroads, we take a peek,
Decide if we want ice cream or speak.
Lemonade stands and puppy dogs,
Adventure awaits, in laughter logs.

Maps scribbled on the backs of hands,
Lead us through whimsical lands.
Every turn, a surprise in view,
Hungry for giggles, we've caught a clue.

Tipsy paths and zigzag routes,
With mischief lurking, joy enroute.
Let's spin in circles, throw our fears,
Together we'll summon magic cheers.

Navigating the Sea of Significance

With a map that's upside down,
And a compass that points to clown,
I sail past the islands of doubt,
Laughing at what life's about.

The waves of wisdom crash and play,
As gulls squawk, 'Hooray, hooray!'
In the harbor of silly schemes,
People chase their wildest dreams.

A mermaid offers me a snack,
Saying, 'Fret not, there's no way back!'
I bite into a cake of fate,
And giggle at what makes us great.

My ship's crew made of rubber ducks,
Floating by, just testing luck,
Dancing around life's endless tide,
Throwing fish and laughs wide!

Collecting Fragments of Truth

With a net made of glitter and fluff,
I catch thoughts like they're bits of puff,
Understanding is hard to define,
Especially when truth tastes like brine.

I wander the fields of obvious lies,
Hunting for truths in a world of pies,
Each slice a lesson, warm and sweet,
Finding wisdom under my feet.

Sifting through pockets of worn-out shoes,
I gather up all the quirky clues,
A riddle wrapped in a soggy sock,
Laughing as I check my clock.

Each pebble holds stories of yore,
Sparkling truths and so much more,
Giggling as I clutch my trove,
Ready to share what truth can't prove.

Journeys Through Forgotten Realms

I wandered off into the mist,
Where logic and nonsense coexist,
Chasing shadows that dance on air,
With socks that still have flair.

A dragon named Dave guards a door,
Revealing secrets from days of yore,
With a wink and a silly grin,
He shouts, 'Your journey can begin!'

Through valleys of giggles and frowns,
I met the king of the upside-downs,
He shared a banana peel's great worth,
Proving laughter brings joy to earth.

At the edge of this wondrous terrain,
Wisdom flows like a light-hearted rain,
Spinning tales on loops of fun,
In forgotten realms, I've just begun!

Gems of Insight Along the Way

Beneath a tree with ten-foot fruit,
I pick gems of insight, cute and astute,
They glitter brightly in shades of cheer,
Saying, 'Life's puzzle is nothing to fear!'

A squirrel with glasses points the way,
To treasures hidden in bright display,
With every nut, another hint,
To understand what makes us sprint.

I stumble upon a wise old shoe,
It chuckles, 'You've much to pursue!'
'Walk carefully on each shiny stone,
For wisdom's a dance, not a loan.'

As I waltz with my newfound grace,
Witty thoughts sprout in every space,
Collecting laughter, love, and play,
Gems of insight come what may!

Whispers of the Infinite

In the search for treasures rare,
I found a sock beneath my chair.
Tangled dreams and silly hats,
A quest that's full of goofy chats.

Unicorns on pogo sticks,
Chasing happiness with silly tricks.
A rubber chicken in my quest,
Laughter leads me to the best.

Maps drawn in crayon and glue,
With arrows pointing to the zoo.
Life's oddities make me smile,
As I roam the wacky mile.

Footprints in whipped cream I see,
Leading me to ice cream and glee.
In the hunt for joy, I run,
Finding fun is number one!

Chronicles of the Soul's Pursuit

Once I searched for golden keys,
Underneath the buzzing bees.
But all I found was mashed-up cake,
And a tiny dancing snake.

Questing for wisdom, I tripped,
On a banana peel, I slipped.
The wise owl just laughed and said,
"Keep your eyes on what's ahead!"

In the whimsical garden maze,
I lost myself in a silly daze.
Balloons were floating through the air,
Each one burst, who had time to care?

Through puddles of jelly I gleefully went,
Laughing hard, I felt quite bent.
The universe's game is cheeky and sly,
Searching joy is my alibi!

The Compass of Inner Discovery

With a compass made of candy canes,
I wandered through the silly plains.
Every direction led to glee,
In the land of pranks and harmony.

Silly songs danced in the breeze,
Laughter echoed like buzzing bees.
I found a wizard in the trees,
Who offered me some magic cheese.

Maps drawn in melted chocolate,
A compass spin, oh what a plot!
Climbing mountains of fluffy marshmallows,
Sliding down like playful gallows.

The quest for giggles never ends,
With quirky creatures, my best friends.
In this pursuit, I take a stand,
Fun and laughter hand in hand!

Parables in the Playground of Life

Swinging high among the clouds,
I laughed out loud with giggling crowds.
Slides made of twinkling stars,
A journey painted with candy bars.

Searching for wisdom in treehouse heights,
Jumping through the joyful nights.
Merry-go-rounds with dizzy spins,
In this playground, everyone wins!

A fortune cookie told me jokes,
And bubble gum, it always pokes.
I found a treasure chest of cheer,
With every giggle, I persevere.

Life's absurdities make me grin,
In this hunt, it's fun to win.
With each tickle and silly prank,
I dive into the joy, no need to thank!

The Art of Discovery

In search of treasures, we roam the park,
With maps made of chicken scratch and a flashlight spark.

A sandwich for bait, what a curious plight,
We'll find something grand by the end of the night.

Unraveled mysteries in a cereal box,
Could it be magic or just old socks?
The quest takes a turn with silly surprise,
Maybe gold is found, or just leftover fries.

We stumble on wonders, a bottle cap prize,
Laughing at fortune, surprise in our eyes.
A flat tire leads to a treasure so sweet,
Turns out it's just gum stuck under a seat.

Chasing the silly and dancing with fate,
Collecting odd findings that make our hearts great.
With each little giggle, we savor the ride,
The art of discovery—the joy in our stride.

Secrets Beneath the Surface

Beneath the garden lies tales to uncover,
A sock with a story, a prized plot to discover.
Worms whisper secrets, beneath the thick dirt,
Of gnomes on adventures and pirates that flirt.

Lifting the stones, oh what do we see?
A fortune cookie, cracked open by me!
"Your luck is like pudding, all wobbly and round,"
We laugh as we search, feeling joy all around.

Each whispered secret, a giggle ignites,
The tales of the creatures in swirling moonlight.
A legend of lost toys, and quests of old chairs,
We find joy in the journey, and no one despairs.

Under the bushes, we dig and we dive,
Finding goofy things that help us feel alive.
The surface may shimmer, but the fun's in the quest,
In secrets and laughter, we are blessed!

Beyond the Veil of Illusion

Behind the curtain lies wonders galore,
With magic and mayhem, and laughter outpour.
We peek through the veil, and what do we find?
A rubber chicken, and a shoelace entwined.

The mysteries deepen with each playful glance,
As we flail like gnomes in a whimsical dance.
Illusions of sanity swirl in the air,
But the fun is real, like a cat on a chair.

When light bends just right, the shadows go wild,
Taking us back to the innocence of a child.
A whirl of confusion, but who really knows?
With giggles and keels, our imaginations grow.

We laugh at reflections, distortions of glee,
Chasing the echoes, setting our minds free.
Beyond what we see, lies laughter and cheer,
For life's just a joke, and we're all in on here.

Tracing the Lineage of Life

In the family tree, there's a branch that's askew,
An uncle who juggles, and a cousin named Boo.
Tracing our roots, what a curious game,
Turns out great auntie's a little insane!

With stories retold, each character winks,
A great grandpa's waiting in clown pants, it stinks!
We dig through the photos, look what we see—
A pet rock was famous, back in '83!

The legends of yore add giggles and grins,
With knick-knacks and trinkets that cause silly spins.
Every quirky tale ignites a warm chuckle,
As we trace our lineage, with all this muckle.

So here's to the humor in family lore,
The tales filled with laughter, that we all do adore.
Finding joy in our past, a ridiculous plight,
Tracing the lineage, with love, what a sight!

Notes to the Cosmos

I wrote a note and sent it up,
With a stamp made from my favorite cup.
The stars replied with giggles bright,
Saying, 'No refunds! You're not quite right.'

I asked them where my socks had gone,
They said, 'Check the wash, then move along.'
They laugh at plans that seem so grand,
While sipping tea in a cosmic band.

I scribbled dreams on paper moons,
And wished for snacks beneath the tunes.
They sent me cheese with a side of bliss,
But noted that dessert's still amiss.

So if you send your hopes and dreams,
Beware of cosmic jokes and screams.
For in this vast and silly dance,
Life's but a wacky fortune glance.

Unlocking the Vaults of Emotion

I found a key to happiness' door,
But opened up a closet of chores.
There sat a cat with a puzzled frown,
Sipping tea while I searched around.

I turned the lock on disappointment,
And out came snacks with a sweet appointment.
My heart did somersaults and splits,
As candy rained down in joyful bits.

I cracked the vault of shiny dreams,
But all I found were old ice creams.
The flavors danced, a sticky mess,
An emotional rollercoaster of silly stress.

So here's a secret, listen well,
Unlock with laughter, and all will gel.
For feelings come in wobbly waves,
And humor's the key that always saves.

Fables of the Seeker

Once there was a seeker on a quest,
Who thought that wisdom was the best.
He searched for truth in cookie crumbs,
And listened for love in shaking drums.

He found a sage beneath a tree,
But all she spoke was about her tea.
'Life's like a kettle, boiling and steep,
Sip slowly, and don't forget to weep.'

He chased a rainbow, fell in a puddle,
And from the mud grew a wise little cuddle.
It whispered softly to laugh and play,
For meaning comes in the silliest way.

So if you seek with open eyes,
Don't miss the fun—not just the wise.
For in the grins and goofy pursuits,
You'll find the treasure that truly roots.

Pursuit of the Uncommon Thread

In a land where socks go missing,
Happiness wears just one shoe.
Chasing rainbows made of garlic,
While searching for the lost and blue.

A duck with dreams of winning gold,
Perches on a teetering chair.
Digging through the garden's old,
For treasures that aren't even there.

With mystery maps and junkyard finds,
We stumble through our daily quest.
An orange peel that speaks in rhymes,
Oh, this nonsense makes us jest!

The truth appears in funny shapes,
In every twist, a giggle blooms.
Life's a circus, full of scrapes,
As we rummage through the rooms!

Echoing Footfalls of Understanding

The keys to joy are oddly shaped,
Like puzzles made for mice, not men.
Giggles echo, tales escaped,
As we play hopscotch with a hen.

We chase the sun with chocolate hats,
While searching for forgotten socks.
The fish can dance, the cat just chats,
Wonders lie behind the rocks.

Each clue we find is soaked in giggles,
Like pickles lost in summer heat.
Our laughter leaps and wobbles, jiggles,
As we dart from street to street.

In this maze of joyous play,
Every step reveals a smile.
With silly hats and shades of gray,
Together, we walk every mile!

Chasing Shadows of Significance

Riding cows that moo in rhythm,
We leap into the evening dusk.
Hunting ghosts of wit and wisdom,
Dancing with a pie that's just.

The treasure chest filled up with jokes,
Stashed behind a door of fame.
We gamble laughs where folly pokes,
And find absurdity's true name.

Bouncing on some rubber springs,
We twirl amidst the vines and weeds.
The meaning floats on feathered wings,
A quest that fills our silly needs.

Each moment sparks with carefree flair,
As shadows leap from tree to tree.
A wild chase flows through the air,
Where laughter sets our spirits free!

Whispers of Existence

In gardens where the daisies sing,
We search for wisdom in the breeze.
A frog recites a haiku king,
While pondering life's quirky tease.

Balloon animals fly by the moon,
Wishing stars made out of cheese.
The heartbeats start a funky tune,
As we swing on silly trees.

With ice cream cones that sprout a tale,
And conversations with a spoon,
We follow trails where giggles sail,
In hopes of finding something soon.

Each whisper holds a quirky truth,
Hidden within laughter's embrace.
The hunt is sweet, a jesting sleuth,
No rush to finish this good race!

Chasing Fleeting Moments

In a park with ice cream stains,
We chase the sun through silly games.
A frog in a hat jumps to the beat,
Laughing, we dance, skip, and repeat.

Lemonade stands with splashy spills,
A race to fill our paper wills.
Fleeting moments tucked away tight,
As shadows grow long in fading light.

The Alchemy of Meaning

In a world of socks, mismatched delight,
We brew our dreams on a whim, just right.
A sprinkle of chaos, a dash of cheer,
Turning mundane into something dear.

A wizard with glasses, a spoon in hand,
Conjures up laughter across the land.
Gold is just silly, but joy's the prize,
When you toast to life with wide-open eyes.

Epochs of Elation and Sorrow

A daydream born on a roller coaster,
Where giggles flutter and hearts get poster.
We cherish the highs like candy on tongues,
And shuffle through lows with twisted puns.

In waltzes of joy and dips of despair,
We all juggle life, with flair and a scare.
Like popcorn that bursts at its funny seams,
We shop for laughter and barter our dreams.

Layers of Existence

Like onions with flavors, we peel and laugh,
Searching for layers, we cut the path.
Each slice reveals what's hidden inside,
With layers of giggles, we won't run and hide.

A ticklish tickle, a whimsical sting,
Finding the humor in small, silly things.
As we slice through the layers, what do we find?
A cosmic joke shared, a joyous mind!

The Books in the Forest

In a forest of tales, I found quite a tome,
Where trees whispered words and led me back home.
The rabbits read chapters, the birds sang the lines,
While squirrels plotted plots with these secret designs.

A mushroom, a sage, shared wisdom on leaves,
Said, "Life's full of giggles, so never believe."
With each turn of page, a new riddle popped,
And I laughed so hard, my worries all dropped.

I stumbled on stories of dragons that bake,
And how to make coffee from an acorn cake.
But as night softly fell and the pages grew dim,
I chased fireflies home, humming wordy whim.

Those books in the forest, who knew they could teach,
A nonsense adventure that lingered in speech.
With each quirky fable, a lesson so grand,
That maybe, just maybe, it's all in the plan.

Soul Searching in Silence

In silence, I searched for a morsel of truth,
Found a sock and a sandwich, I swear, that's the proof.
A whispering breeze had a riddle in tune,
Said, "Search underwater, perhaps with a spoon."

I tripped on my thoughts, they dived off the path,
They laughed at my jaw when I lost my own math.
With each awkward stumble, I pondered the game,
Is life just a circus? Am I to blame?

A turtle rolled by, wearing glasses of gold,
Claimed that wisdom is found where the laughter unfolds.
Yet, there's a banana peel here for my despair,
I slip and I giggle, life's a comedic affair.

So, I wade through my musings with giggles and glee,
A soul-searching mission that's silly, you see.
The quiet holds laughter, and maybe that's it,
To gain all the joy through a whimsical fit.

Notes from the Edge of Existence

At the edge of existence, I scribbled a note,
On a napkin, I wrote what I hoped wouldn't float.
A comedy sketch that I hoped would inspire,
About daydreaming lizards who all aspired.

They gathered for meetings in socks and old hats,
Debating life's meaning over chocolate-spiced chats.
With punchlines delivered in rhythms of cheer,
They showed that existence is wacky and dear.

Each line that I penned was a tickle of fun,
Bright insights unveiled while I balanced on pun.
There's laughter in questions, that much is for sure,
And wisdom in jokes that are silly but pure.

So here is my note from the edge and beyond,
Where laughter prevails and the silly respond.
Let's celebrate nonsense, with giggles galore,
For notes filled with joy are what I treasure more.

Reverberations of the Eternal

In echoes of laughter, I found my sweet voice,
It bounced off the mountains, making the best noise.
Fluffy clouds with laughter floated above,
Whispering tidbits about life and its love.

A giraffe with a trumpet serenaded the wind,
While hippos debated if they'd wear a skin blend.
Each ripple of chuckles across valleys did sing,
That joy is the essence of most everything.

The eternal's a party, with snacks on the side,
With karaoke sessions that we can't let slide.
So gather your friends, bring a hat for some flair,
For the echoes of laughter are meant to share!

In reverberations, the universe cares,
About giggles and fun, and the silly affairs.
So life's greatest treasure, I must now pronounce,
Is the joy that we find, let's all share the bounce!

The Heart's Hidden Compendium

In a box of lost socks, I found a clue,
A rubber chicken, and a frog in a shoe.
Laughter echoes in the vibrant air,
A quest for giggles, embark if you dare!

A map made of jellybeans led me astray,
With each sticky step, I laughed all the way.
Unruly adventures in my quaint little mind,
The treasure is silly, the funniest kind!

With a riddle from a cat, perched up high,
"What flies without wings?" it asked with a sigh.
It's time for a chuckle, so let's take a peek,
The answer is laughter, so joyful, so sleek!

In a jungle of coupons, I swing from a vine,
Looking for nonsense, oh, this is divine.
The heart's hidden gems, so quirky, so sweet,
In the midst of the chaos, we're dancing on feet!

A Symphony of Curiosities

A dog wore my hat, looking quite grand,
Conducting the chaos with a paw in the band.
The drum's just a catnap, the bass is a shoe,
A symphony's forming, oh what will they do?

Dancing of vegetables, the carrots take lead,
While turnips and radishes follow their creed.
As onions play trumpets, I chuckle a lot,
A humorous journey in this whimsical plot!

A kazoo serenade from a wise old owl,
It quips and it hoots, giving laughter a growl.
With a brass and a woodwind, the carrots rejoice,
In this funny melody, we all find our voice!

In the end, we find joy in the quirkiest sounds,
Every laugh, every giggle, a treasure abounds.
A symphony of oddities, we hum with delight,
Together we dance through the marvelous night.

Finding Patterns in Chaos

In the mess of my room, I see socks on the floor,
A puzzle of oddities, there's always more!
The cat joins the hunt, with a flick of its tail,
Together we discover that chaos can sail!

A sandwich with pickles, a donut on top,
With sprinkles and jelly, it just cannot stop!
Pants worn like a hat, oh, the joy that it brings,
In the chaos we chuckle, while life sings its flings!

Finding patterns in hiccups, in laughter we dive,
Each giggle a jewel, so sparkling, alive.
The dance of the silly, the charm of the odd,
In chaos we find what makes us applaud!

So gather your treasures, each knickknack, each toy,
In the muddle of madness, let's revel with joy.
For in finding the fun, in the wacky and wild,
We learn from the chaos, each grown-up, each child!

The Compass of Contentment

With a compass of giggles, I wander around,
Each chuckle a marker, in joy I am found.
Through landscapes of laughter, my spirit takes flight,
Finding bliss in the nonsense, oh what a sight!

A snack made of pickles and chocolate so sweet,
The taste of contentment is often a treat.
With a unicorn blender, creating a whirl,
The compass is spinning: let's dance, give a twirl!

A map drawn in crayon, with paths of delight,
We chase after rainbows that sparkle at night.
In the journey of whimsy, with friends by my side,
The compass of laughter, our giggly guide!

So wherever it points, let joy be your aim,
For the pursuit of the funny is never the same.
In the heart of contentment, we find our own way,
With smiles as the currency—come join the sway!

Fragments of Infinity

In the attic of thought, I found a sock,
Does it hold wisdom? Or just a clock?
With every tick, it tells me to snack,
A snack of wisdom, who's got my back?

I chased a paperclip, it flew like a bird,
In its shiny gleam, I found my word.
Was it nonsense? Just clutter I seek,
Or the solution to life? Oh, how unique!

Old cereal boxes whisper tales,
Of adventures in milk, of glorious fails.
In breakfast, I find both joy and strife,
Who knew crunchiness held the key to life?

So I stash these fragments, odd and bright,
In the drawers of dreams, hidden from sight.
With a goofy grin, I carry my load,
Laughter and chaos, on this strange road.

Kaleidoscope of Encounters

I met a cat who wore a bowtie,
Sipped on tea and told me why.
He said, 'Life's a game, just dance and twirl,'
Then he pranced away, what a whirl!

A llama on a unicycle sped by,
Yelling, 'Join the circus, reach for the sky!'
I laughed so hard, I tripped on my shoe,
In this crazy world, there's always a cue.

With jellybeans raining from the trees,
I caught a few, as I laughed with glee.
The squirrels joined in, tapping their feet,
In this jungle of fun, they'd never retreat.

Every encounter, a vibrant hue,
A color of chaos, bright and true.
Life's a kaleidoscope, twist it just right,
Each turn brings a giggle, pure delight.

The Narratives We Weave

With stories in my pocket, I stroll along,
Each step a verse, life's silly song.
I met a dog who spoke in rhyme,
He said, 'Tell your tales; it's playtime!'

A penguin in a tutu tapped his feet,
Claiming he won the world's best tweet.
With every quirk, he danced and quacked,
In this quirky play, no truth is lacked.

A sandwich whispered secrets of the past,
Between the bread, life zips by fast.
I chuckled at mustard, bold in his pride,
He tossed around wisdom, quite the ride!

So we weave our narratives, laugh and sigh,
With each odd thread, like clouds in the sky.
In this tapestry of fun and cheer,
We find our tales, crystal clear!

Tides of Reflection

I gazed at a puddle, a mirror so clear,
It winked at me, 'Come laugh, my dear!'
In its depths, I saw a fish with a hat,
Remind me again, what's life all about?

The tides of reflection, they ebb and flow,
Sometimes I'm wise, sometimes a show.
Like a rubber duck sailing on foam,
I ponder life's mysteries far from home.

A seagull swooped down, surveying the beach,
With a squawk, he said, 'Life's within reach!'
I tossed him some crumbs, he guffawed and flew,
'Catch me a wave, let's start something new!'

So I dance with the ripples, giggles arise,
In this splashy vision, no need for disguise.
With laughter as my compass and joy as my map,
I navigate the tides, no time for a nap!

Hidden in Plain Sight

Under the couch, my sock lies,
A treasure map, much to my surprise.
The clues are scrambled, but I don't mind,
Happiness hidden, just waiting to find.

A cookie jar whispers secrets untold,
In each crinkle and crack, treasures unfold.
Searching for meaning, in crumbs on the floor,
Turns out my purpose was snacking galore!

Lost in the fridge, that leftover stew,
Turns into wisdom, who knew it could do?
I follow the odors, a breadcrumb brigade,
Finding delight in the mess that I've made.

So laugh as you journey, don't take it too far,
The meaning may lurk in a chocolate-filled jar.
The quest can be silly, just follow your nose,
In the search for your truth, may your laughter expose.

Signposts of the Heart

A signpost says 'left' but I go to the right,
Stumbling upon a pizza delight.
Navigating life with a fork in my hand,
Each slice is a lesson, almost unplanned.

In the park, I spot a squirrel with flair,
He scolds me for not sharing my pair.
With every nut he buries in the ground,
Is a giggle that echoes, the joy that I've found.

Tiny balloons float, announcing some fun,
Life's silly moments, in the warmth of the sun.
A dance in the fountain, a splash on my shoe,
Chasing around the meaning, we laugh 'til we're blue.

So take to the roads where whimsy prevails,
In every odd corner, let laughter unveil.
Signposts may point, but your heart knows the way,
In the puzzle of life, it's fun every day.

Revelations on the Journey

I once found a shoe that belonged to my cat,
Revelations arise from the curious spat.
With each step I take, I trip on a toy,
Life's quirky surprises bring mischievous joy.

Maps all around me, but who needs them now?
A detour with llamas, I'm wandering how.
They stare with such wisdom, they nibble and chew,
Teaching me lessons, with their cute little view.

I find bits of wisdom in junk shops and stands,
Old trinkets that whisper of faraway lands.
And in every odd item, a laughter-filled clue,
The search for the grand can just start with a shoe.

So gather your mishaps, make fun of the strife,
In the revelations, you'll find the fun life.
Chase all the giggles wherever they flee,
In the journey of laughter, come wander with me.

The Riddle of Our Existence

Why did the chicken cross the road?
To escape from questions, her spirit bestowed.
In each crossing of paths, we ponder the dare,
Laughter's the answer because life's never fair.

In the garden of chaos, weeds grow in lines,
But amongst the confusion, the sunshine shines.
We question the shadows while dancing in light,
Finding riddles where giggles take flight.

With cupcakes as currency, we barter our dreams,
In the land of absurd where nothing's as it seems.
A riddle unraveled with sprinkles on top,
Can a quest for the funny ever really stop?

So solve the conundrum, don't scratch your own head,
In the riddle of laughter, we're all gently led.
The meaning's elusive, but here's the decree:
Life's best revelations are sweet as a spree.

Discovering the Map of Wonder

With a magnifying glass, I search the ground,
Finding clues where laughter's found.
A rubber chicken leads the way,
To a treasure chest of silly play.

Follow the puns and riddles galore,
Each step I take opens another door.
A map scribbled in crayon hues,
Marks the spot for ice cream snooze.

Giggles echo as I trot along,
With a dancing cat to a ukulele song.
Life's puzzle pieces, bright and strange,
Add a twist to the playful exchange.

Underneath the goofy hat,
I find joy in simple chat.
Through laughter, I discover the fun,
The map to wonder has just begun!

Footprints of the Soul

Tiny footprints scatter wide,
Leading me to joy, not to hide.
A duck in sunglasses waddles by,
Sipping tea and waving high.

In this dance of goofy stride,
I slip on joy, no need to slide.
With each footprint, lessons spill,
Who knew life could be this thrill?

I chase after a rainbow cat,
Who speaks in rhymes and wears a hat.
Each step reveals a chuckling gig,
In puddles, I discover the big!

In the game of silly chase,
There's a smile on every face.
Footprints lead to laughter's call,
A treasure found, surprising all!

Searching for Silver Linings

Caffeine-stained maps in hand,
I quest for gigs across the land.
Under clouds of whipped cream fluff,
I gather silver — never enough!

Glimmers hide in coffee spills,
I scoop them up with random thrills.
In every fumble, I find delight,
Chasing laughter until the night.

With a spoon of sugar and basil too,
Every silver lining's something new.
A twist of fate, a happy surprise,
Flies wearing ties and donut pies.

In the bowl of life's great stew,
There's always a wacky clue.
So I search high, I search low,
For silver lines that brighten the show!

Finding the Golden Thread

In a world of odd textiles, I roam,
To find golden threads that lead me home.
A cat in boots and socks of plaid,
Winks at me—oh, isn't that rad?

I tug at strings of laughter bright,
Each yank reveals a new delight.
With a needle, I sew up fun,
Patchwork giggles for everyone!

Through tangled yarn and colors bold,
The stories of silliness unfold.
A scarf of jokes, a hat with cheer,
Every stitch whispers, "Come over here!"

So I gather threads, each a tease,
Woven with joy, stitched with ease.
In this tapestry, I glide and tread,
With all my heart, the threads I spread!

Unlocking Fate's Toolbox

In a shed of old tools, I do roam,
Searching for wisdom in a rusty comb.
A hammer of laughter, a wrench of cheer,
Unlocking the secrets that always appear.

With screwdrivers spinning and pliers that twist,
I find the key notes that I can't resist.
A toolbox of fate with a quirky design,
Hilarity hides in the mundane line.

Buried Treasures of Truth

I dug in the garden for pearls made of gold,
Found socks from last summer, or so I'm told.
A shovel of giggles, the dirt piled high,
Unearthing the nonsense that made me cry.

X marks the spot where the humor laid bare,
Amongst weeds and thistles, there's laughter to share.
The treasure is laughter, the maps are absurd,
Searching for truths in the quirkiest word.

The Hunt for Cosmic Clarity

With a net made of dreams, I wander the skies,
Catching the wisps of celestial lies.
Stars chuckle brightly, their twinkling a jest,
In the cosmic bazaar, I'm truly a guest.

I barter with comets for wisdom and glee,
Trading my thoughts with a buzz from a bee.
Galaxies giggle as planets collide,
Jokes in the orbits where laughter resides.

Threads of Infinity

I knit with the yarn of the universe wide,
Pulling on strings, with the cosmos as guide.
Laughter is woven in every tight stitch,
Spinning the fabric without any hitch.

A tapestry grand, with colors so bright,
Infinity teases in patterns of light.
Each loop is a giggle, each knot a surprise,
Crafting a quilt that can open our eyes.

Treasures of Transcendence

In a garden of socks, what do we find?
A wealth of lost change, and a goose that's blind.
Picking up trinkets that make no sense,
Like a spoon with a story, or a cat with a fence.

Wandering through drawers, we shout with glee,
A forgotten game, it's Monopoly!
The thrill of the hunt, each find so absurd,
Like a rubber chicken, or a singing bird.

Under the couch, a mysterious lump,
It's not just the dust but a rubbery clump.
We chuckle and giggle at treasures so grand,
A map to the gummy bears, oh isn't life planned?

As we tally our loot, with grins ear to ear,
It's not just the finds, but the hilarious cheer.
Through chaos and laughter, our search never ends,
In a world full of nonsense, we're all the best friends.

Clues Beneath the Stars

A starry night sky, what's that up above?
Is it a UFO, or a lost little dove?
With binoculars handy, we squint at the light,
Hoping to find some strange, silly sight.

Under blanket fort castles, we search high and low,
Searching for clues in the popcorn we throw.
A map sketched in crumbs, with an arrow so bold,
Leading to dreams that feel funny and old.

The constellations giggle, the Milky Way grins,
As we chase our wild fantasies, hoping for wins.
From Venus to Mars, the quest is our spark,
Finding laughter in moments that dance in the dark.

With each funny mishap, we write down our tales,
Each clue that we gather, as laughter prevails.
Beneath the night sky, we're on a great roll,
For in every starlit giggle, we unlock our soul.

Unraveling the Tapestry of Being

Threads of existence tangled up tight,
We laugh at the patterns as best as we might.
Unraveling questions with each silly pull,
Like a cat with a yarn ball, our joy's ever full.

Colors collide in a whimsical dance,
As we twirl through existence, giving thought a chance.
The fabric of life, it's quirky and grand,
With pockets of wisdom and jellybeans at hand.

Each knot that we tug leads to sidesplitting lore,
A patchwork of oddities, who could ask for more?
Holes filled with riddles and whimsical fables,
Knitting our laughs into tangled-up tables.

And as we create this bizarre tapestry,
The humor in life's woven intricacy.
In stitches of laughter and giggles so sweet,
We find joy in the chaos, oh what a treat!

Quest for Echoes of Purpose

With maps made of pizza and plans full of zest,
We set off on journeys to find out the best.
In caves of confusion, we search for a clue,
Each echo we hear makes us giggle anew.

Chasing after shadows, we play hide and seek,
A quest for the questions, it's fun and unique.
With compasses spinning, and laughter in hand,
Each step a new riddle, completely unplanned.

We hop on a trampoline, bounce into the air,
Searching for meaning in our wild, joyous flair.
Like explorers of nonsense, with treasures to claim,
Every bounce tells a story, it's all just a game.

As day turns to night, our laughter won't cease,
We find joy in the jumbled, an echo of peace.
The quest's not for answers, but the joy that we seek,
In echoes of giggles, it's truest mystique.

The Clockwork of Dreams

Tick tock, the gears they spin,
Chasing the laughs where they have been.
A rubber chicken, a dancing cat,
These silly sights make the heart go splat!

Counting wishes on a starry night,
Each one giggles, 'What a delight!'
With a wink and a jig, they slip away,
Dreamland's treasures are game for play!

Look at the clouds, such curious forms,
A ship, a duck, a hat that swarms.
In this whimsy, we find our way,
Through chuckles and wonders, come what may!

So twirl around in the grand parade,
Life's daft puzzles, unafraid.
With every glance, there's joy and cheer,
Let's dance through dreams, year by year!

Recall of Forgotten Journeys

In dusty drawers, the maps are tossed,
With doodles and snacks, we're never lost.
A cereal box, a compass made,
Led us to lands unafraid!

Remember the trip to the kitchen stage?
Where snacks were treasures, we'd laugh, we'd rage.
The fridge was a portal, the pantry a cave,
With each bite of cookie, we'd feel so brave!

Finding the socks that danced with glee,
Two mismatched pals, wild and free.
Off to the land of the laundry pile,
Where every adventure brings a smile!

So here's to the journeys we often forget,
The giggles, the snacks, we can't regret.
With each little whim, we boldly roam,
In every silly moment, we feel at home!

The Artifacts of Awareness

Look at my rock, it's shaped like a shoe,
A relic from walks that I never knew.
The silly sketches of monsters grand,
Artefacts from the trips, so unplanned!

A cereal spoon with wisdom to share,
It whispers secrets of breakfast flair.
The laughter spills over the morning bowl,
Every crunchy bite, it fills the soul!

A rubber band made of dreams untold,
To stretch the limits of brave and bold.
Tying up thoughts like wild balloons,
Floating above with joyous tunes!

So gather the bits that make you smile,
From spoons to rocks, it's all worthwhile.
In every chuckle, we find our way,
Awareness unwrapped, come out to play!

Harvesting Wisdom from Experience

In a garden of giggles, we plant our seeds,
Watered by laughter, it's all that it needs.
With a shovel of mishaps, discoveries meet,
Each blunder's a hoe, making life sweet!

To weed out the worries, we bring in the light,
And dance with the daisies, all day and night.
Cactus hugs and daisy chains,
In this wild garden, joy remains!

Come taste the fruits of our labored hours,
A pie made of dreams, a dance that empowers.
With every misstep, we stumble and twirl,
Sharing the magic of our crazy world!

So harvest the joy from each little chance,
With giggles and grins, we join in the dance.
In this patch of wonder, we'll always find,
Wisdom grows best when it's silly and kind!

www.ingramcontent.com/pod-product-compliance
Lightning Source LLC
Chambersburg PA
CBHW071830160426
43209CB00003B/260